PowerPoint Essentials

By

David K. Ewen, M.Ed.

Forest Academy
www.ForestAcademy.org

ISBN-13: 978-1497597709
ISBN-10: 1497597706

PowerPoint is the property of Microsoft

www.ForestAcademy.org

David K. Ewen, M.Ed.

Introduction

I wrote this book in a few hours with the intention of being a quick starter guide and a general introduction to PowerPoint.

This book has been used as a study guide for a class I teach at Forest Academy called "PowerPoint Essentials". It follows my first book on an element of Microsoft Office called "Excel Essentials"

You will have enough information that serves as a strong platform to learn more. To use the expression, you will learn in a few short pages enough to be "dangerous".

This book is a simple direct to the point presentation of how to use PowerPoint to make impressive looking presentation with animation and narration. You'll get to know all the fancy techniques in a few pages.

With what you learn in this book, you will have the ability to intuitively learn other topics on your own that is not covered in this book. You'll have enough understanding to become a PowerPoint expert.

David K. Ewen, M.Ed.
Forest Academy
April 2014

Resources

Here are resources from Microsoft

- www.PowerPoint.com

- support.microsoft.com

- office.microsoft.com

- portal.microsoftonline.com

Keys

There are keys that are important to run powerpoint.

★ **F5 key** - Start presentation mode.

★ **Page Down** - Move Forward

★ **Page Up** - Move Backward

★ **ESC key** - End presentation mode

Toolbars

There are 11 ribbons of tools or 11 toolbars.
They are selected by choosing one of the
following:

- FILE
- HOME
- INSERT
- DESIGN
- TRANSITIONS
- ANIMATIONS
- SLIDE SHOW
- REVIEW
- VIEW
- ADD-INS

File Toolbar

The FILE toolbar allows you to:

➜   NEW - Create a new document

➜   OPEN - Open an existing saved document

➜   SAVE - Save current open document

➜   SAVE AS - Save in a different format or name

➜   PRINT - Print document

➜   SHARE- Share online

➜   EXPORT - Export to PDF

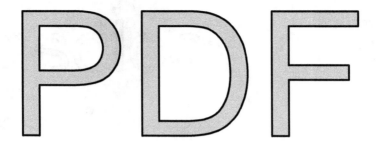

By selecting **file** and then **export**, you can create a PDF file that is perfect for printing and emailing.

The "file" option is the same one used for saving the file and printing the file.

A PDF file is good to send documents that have a nice presentation format and can't be changed.

The ability to create a PDF file from a PPT is for web based documents.

Other Ribbon Toolbars

Each section of the ribbon has a section name at the bottom and is separated by a vertical line. The example below show the sections "Clipboard" and "Slides" in the HOME ribbon.

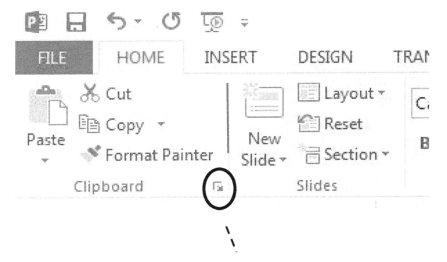

Most sections have a corner arrow that serve as a secondary menu options.

Section of Ribbons

The Tool ribbons with their associated sections are:

→ <u>FILE</u> - New, Open, Save, etc.

→ <u>HOME</u> - Clipboard, Slides, Font, Paragraph, Drawing, Editing

→ <u>INSERT</u> - Slides, Tables, Images, Illustrations, Apps, Links, Comments, Text, Symbols, Media

→ <u>DESIGN</u> - Themes, Variants, Customize

→ <u>TRANSITIONS</u> - Preview, Transitions to This Slide, Timing

→ <u>ANIMATIONS</u> - Preview, Animation, Advanced Animation, Timing

→ <u>SLIDE SHOW</u> - Start Slide Show, Set Up, Monitor

→ <u>REVIEW</u> - Proofing, Language, Comments, Compare

→ <u>VIEW</u> - Presentation View, Master Views, Show, Zoom, Color/GrayScale, Window, Macros

→ <u>ADD-INS</u> - Convert to PDF (tools added)

→ <u>PDF</u> - Save as PDF

Slides

Toolbar ribbon is at the top.

Content is edited here

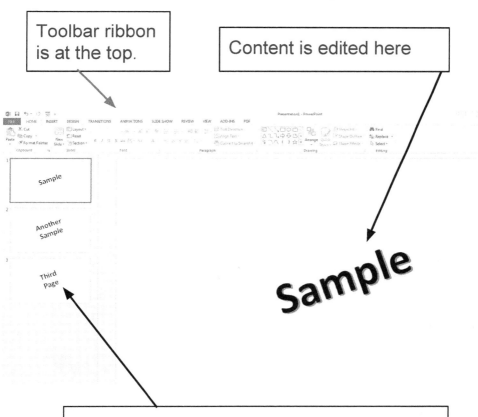

A sort of "table" of contents is here. Each individual slide can be selected for editing.

Layout & Design of Slides

→ Select the **DESIGN** ribbon by selecting DESIGN from the toolbar

→ There are three sections in the DESIGN ribbon:
- Themes,
- Variants,
- Customize

→ Select a Theme from the "***Themes***" section

→ Select colors from the "***Variants***" section

→ Set slide size from "**Customize**" section

→ Other changes from "Customize" section

Word Art

Using Word Art to make a title

➔ Click "INSERT" ribbon

➔ Go to "Text" section

➔ Select Word Art

➔ Click on a desired format

➔ Edit the slide by typing over

◆ **"Your text here"**

➔ With your mouse, drag text to top.

Pictures

To insert images, click INSERT ribbon.

Pictures can added:

→ Images section
- ◆ Upload pictures
- ◆ Add photo albums
- ◆ Screenshot (as is)

→ Illustrations section
- ◆ Shapes (circle, square, lines, etc.)
- ◆ "Smart Art" with several shapes
- ◆ Chart based on excel spreadsheet

Tables

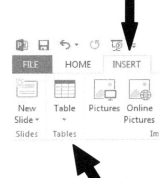

→ Click INSERT ribbon

→ Go to "Tables" Section

→ Click "Table"

→ Determine Rows and Columns

→ Automatically, you will be routed to

    DESIGN ribbon in the "Table Styles"

    section

→ Select Design of table

→ Enter title header in table

→ Enter data in table

Excel

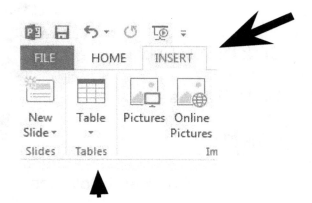

➔ Click INSERT ribbon

➔ Go to "Tables" Section

➔ Select "Excel Spreadsheet"

➔ Drag bottom right corner to size.

➔ Edit Excel Spreadsheet

Excel Chart

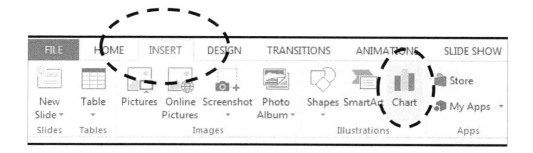

Select the chart to be
represented on the
PowerPoint Slide

Update Excel info to
create chart

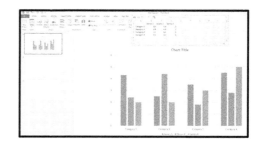

Shapes

Section:
Illustrations

INSERT

Select
"Shapes"

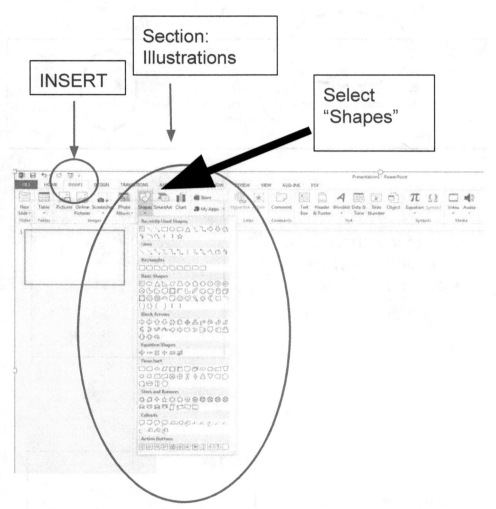

Smart Art
(Custom Shapes)

Smart art allows you to create diagrams that are interconnected with detailed complexities.

The next page shows you how to do this.

Smart Art
(Custom Shapes)

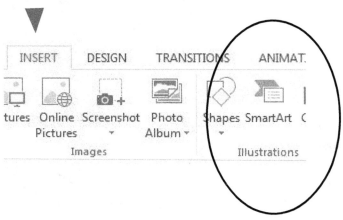

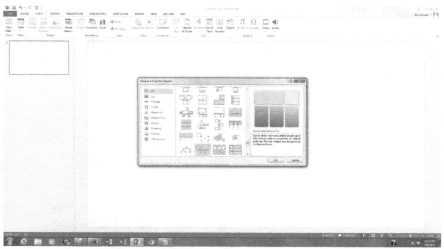

Adding Slides

Select INSERT ribbon and then select "New Slide" found on the far left. Click the down arrow next to the word "New Slide". A box appears. You can create a new slide or duplicate slide(s) by selecting the option at the bottom.

New slide(s)

Duplicate slide(s)

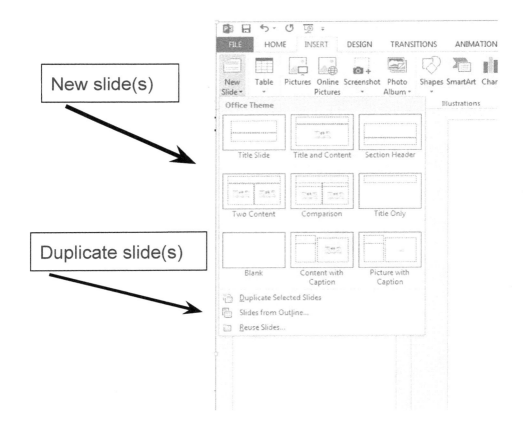

Duplicate Slides

Right click on the selected slide(s)
and select Duplicate Slide.   You
can also delete slide(s) from here.
New slides can be added also.

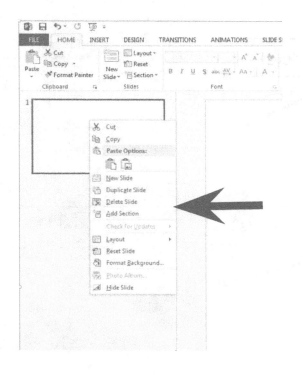

Audio & Video

→ Audio and Video elements can be added.

→ They are activated when clicked on.

→ The audio can be positioned anywhere

→ The video can be sized and positioned.

→ Click **INSERT** ribbon

→ Select **Media** section (far right)

→ Select either **audio** or **video**

→ Audio can be recorded directly or uploaded

→ Video is uploaded

The audio can serve as a manually triggered narration for a slide.

Transition

TRANSITION FROM ONE SLIDE TO THE NEXT

Select the **TRANSITIONS** ribbon.

The Transition Ribbon has <u>three sections</u>

- Preview
- Transitions to This Slide
- Timing

<u>**Preview**</u> is to test a Transition already programmed

<u>**Transitions to This Slide**</u> determines how to transition from one slide to the next

<u>**Timing**</u> is to set the following:

- Sound effect when slides change
- Duration of sound effect
- Advance slide (choose option)
  - On mouse click
  - After amount of time set 00:00:00

Animation

→ Select Element on PPT slide

→ Click ANIMATION Ribbon

→ Select style for animation

→ Test by running PPT

    ◆ Hit F5 (function 5 key)

    ◆ Page UP & DOWN to move

Click on animation	Click animation pane

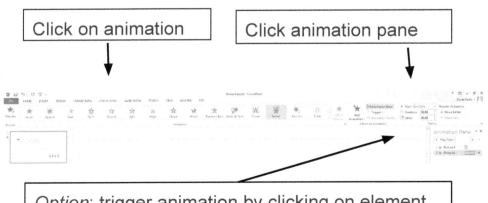

Option: trigger animation by clicking on element

Narration

The narration screens are shown on the next page.

All slides and animations and inserted elements are in place for a completed PowerPoint presentation.

The narration is done as if you are scrolling through a powerpoint while narrating.

When the recorded narration is done, then the powerpoint can be tested by hitting the Function 5 (F5) key and watching the powerpoint play as if it were a movie.

F5 (function 5) - starts the powerpoint

ESC (Escape) exits the powerpoint

Click the **SLIDE SHOW** ribbon
and select **Record Slide Show**,
then select **Start Recording from Beginning...**

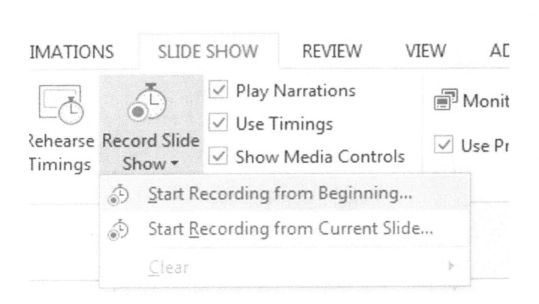

Click **Start Recording** and speak into the mic

Video

A narrated PowerPoint with animations can be saved as a video in MPEG-4 format.

It's easy.

Click **FILE** and then **SAVE AS**.

Save as file type <u>MPEG-4</u> (or another video formatted file type like <u>Windows Media Video</u>.

This file can then be uploaded to video sharing websites and social media.

Resources

Here are resources from Microsoft

- www.PowerPoint.com

- support.microsoft.com

- office.microsoft.com

- portal.microsoftonline.com